BOSS UP

YOUNG ENTREPRENEUR'S GUIDE TO BUSINESS SUCCESS

Marilyn Bryant-Tucker, MBA, EGCBA

BOSS UP: YOUNG ENTREPRENEUR'S GUIDE TO BUSINESS
SUCCESS

Marilyn Bryant-Tucker, MBA, EGCBA

BOSS UP: Young Entrepreneur's Guide to Business Success Copyright@2018 by Marilyn Bryant-Tucker.

Email: info@mbtmarketingsolutions.com Ordering Information:

Quantity sales. Special discounts are available on quantity purchase by corporations, associations, and others. For details, contact the publisher at info@mbtmarketingsolutions.com

Orders by U.S. trade bookstores and wholesalers, please contact MBT Marketing Solutions & Associates Tel: (919) 345-2892 or visitwww.mbtmarketingsolutions.com.

Printed in the United States of America

Book Design and Layout by www.mbtmarketingsolutions.com Marilyn Bryant-Tucker

ISBN-13: 978-1727802641

ISBN-10: 1727802640

DEDICATION

I would like to dedicate this book to my husband, Richard Tucker. I want to thank my handsome husband for being so patient, for sacrificing much of our time together so that I could focus on my gift. Thank you for loving me unconditionally and making me laugh.

I would like to dedicate this book to my Mom for prayers, supporting and encouraging me. You instilled great values and taught your children to have faith and believe. I could not have asked for a better mom or role-model.

For all my loved ones who've gone on to a better life, especially Grand Mother Lillie Mae Bryant, Grand Father James Bryant and Father Fred Dupree-you are always close in heart.

My Father has played a major role in 'who I have become' because he always told me, 'I was beautiful and smart'. I believed that, because my dad told me so.

ACKNOWLEDGMENTS

To my sister Sandra for inspiring me to 'follow my gifts.' I used to work on Saturday's at her Boutique store and learned for the first time that a person can be self-employed and could also become their own boss.

To my sister Teresa for collaborating with me for special event planning.

To Les Long, I truly appreciate providing strategic marketing services for Carolina Comedy. Thank you for organizing great concerts and festivals.

To Michelle Hendricks, thank you for taking time out to listen.

To my clients, you made it possible for me to work on my gift. Lastly, thank you for ordering my book and reading.

CONTENTS

INTRODUCTION

BOSS UP: Young Entrepreneur's Guide to Business Success is a "how to" practical information to start a business with a clean slate. The purpose is to teach the entrepreneurial incline individuals how to start a profitable business.

Studies show that 8 out of 10 businesses failed in their first year. It is saddening how many enterprises go out of business after they launched. The rate at which startups are failing is quite disturbing, and the author of this timely business guide thought it necessary to contribute her quota to give young people the skills needed to make an enduring impact in business.

BOSS UP: Young Entrepreneur's Guide to Business Success is not the usual business book you read. It is an essential entrepreneur companion to succeed in your chosen vocation. After reading this guide, you will be successful every inch of the way.

Running a business may be difficult, but it not for the typical reasons people adduced for the difficulty. Not having enough money might look a plausible reason for failing, but a closer look at the role of money in business will show it is not why startups don't celebrate their first-year anniversary as a successful venture.

BOSS UP: Young Entrepreneur's Guide to Business Success is written by a business savvy who had seen it all when it comes to startups, and her dogged desire to succeed is an inspiration to many who desire success in their business ventures as well.

The young entrepreneurs will learn the following hands-on business information in BOSS UP:

- How to market

- How to brand your company

- How to gain a competitive advantage

- How to reach your target market and win more consumers

- How to set real and realistic short, medium and long-term goals

- Learn how to build your brand and excel

- Learn to turn your gifts, hobbies into a profitable business

The easy to read business guide contains effectual topics that chew on the crux of starting and running a profitable business. The title "Turn Up Your Gifts, like other topics, touched on issues that bring out the entrepreneurial person in the reader. The guide was written to prepare the reader's mind to cope with all stages of doing business. It is a character building expose to dress for the occasion of doing business the proper way. The title "Book Discussion Questions" deals with uniquely answering business-related questions.

After reading BOSS UP, you will gain the skill, knowledge and become a startup master. You can conceptualize a business model and go through the various stages of building a profitable business.

Why should you read BOSS UP?

1. Learn valuable life lessons about business

2. Learn time management, set your schedule and do what you love.

3. Learn business communication and handle presentation like a pro.

4. Learn to build a compelling portfolio that stands out.

When you run a successful business, you will find out that the world of business is not as complicated as it looks. Once you know the tactics and strategy to use, your perception of doing business will change.

BOSS UP isn't a book to take with a pinch of salt because the writer, Marilyn Bryant-Tucker, MBA, EGCBA, is an authority in startups, and after starting and nurturing a couple of businesses herself, the jinx of failure will be broken.

Read BOSS UP with confidence knowing this is all you need to overcome failure in business!

TURN UP YOUR GIFTS

Young people need to be inspired and if parents can see their children's gifts, then they should help them and encourage them, and nurture those gifts. As a child, I had an entrepreneurial spirit; what a gift to possess, naturally! I remember having yard sales, selling M&Ms' and oranges: whatever I could get my little hands onto, I could market and make a success out of it. This was something automatic to my spirit and my nature. I was one of those people that could sell ice to Eskimos'.

We all have special gifting's and abilities unique to ourselves; not everyone can do what you can do. And not everyone will be happy about what you can do and what they cannot do. In fact, you may even have some people who really dislike you because of what you can do, and what they cannot. It's called jealousy. But here's the catch that many people miss . . . they will also have their own talents and abilities that you don't have! It's what they do with them that will either make a success out of them, or a failure. And this is just what I want to talk about with you today.

You can be your own best friend, or your own worst nightmare; and if people are jealous of you and your abilities, then that is not your problem, but theirs. Be sure it doesn't affect you negatively.

If you can play a musical instrument, or solve a math problem in a heartbeat, then do it! If you can catch balls or hit them with ease, then do that! But if you cannot walk a tightrope, or even stay on a horse back for more than a second, then don't!

Follow your heart; do what you can do in the natural with gusto. Let those that can ride a horse, ride a horse. Don't get on your high– horse and grumble about it (pun intended).

Bishop Noel Jones, may have said this . . . "If you don't have any haters, then you are not very gifted." What does that mean? Does that mean . . . if you have no haters, then you have no gifting's? I don't think so: we all have talents! No, I think it's more likely to mean . . . you are not using your gifting's . . . there is no evidence of them. Perhaps you've buried them! What do you think about that?

I remember mom sewing my cloths when I was in middle school and then through college. I would somehow be nominated every year, through my dormitory, for being the best dressed undergraduate at Fayetteville State University. My mom was very gifted; she would see that my sisters, myself and other friends and classmates were well looked after. She operated in her gifting's and it was evident. I would draw out the design and pick out the material, I didn't know that I was becoming a Fashion Designer. Were other girls jealous? I have no doubt!

I never forgot once, when I was at a big event and someone said this . . . what you've got on, is so Phat! I didn't know what that meant, and I could have been quite offended by such a statement; but my friends told me (thank God for friends!) he's saying your outfit is hot! So, work out your gifts, learn what you're good at: and let's make some haters out there! (Oh, and then send them to this book – so they can learn the good stuff that you're learning.)

BEGINNER'S GUIDE TO BRANDING

You are reading right now an easy to follow, snapshot guide to branding, designed to open your eyes to the niceties of branding and business model. Learning the fabric and tissues of branding can be frustrating for the unprepared mind, but this chapter aims at creating the desired attention and awareness of how to approach branding as a beginner and move on to become a versatile business model consultant to take your service to the next level.

Topics to cover

1. Branding defined

2. How branding works

3. Branding elements

4. Building a brand identity

5. Brand voice and visuals

6. Brand applications

Branding Defined

Branding is the idea or image associated with a product, service as de scribed by the name of such idea or product. In other words, branding is the process of empowering a brand to convey a distinct meaning to the audience or market. A brand includes the name, term, symbol, design, slogan and more distinguishing features the brand owner wants the market to associate with the brand and the process by which such identity is created is called branding.

Take for instance, if I call the name of this chapter – Beginner's Guide to Branding, and I go ahead to associate that name with the color red, happiness, and I designed a curvy logo to represent it and define other features… and I go ahead to promote it using various content, marketing channel and strategies. When that name and the entire distinguishing elements sink with the market, and they can associate the multiple characteristics so defined with the brand name… then I have successfully gone through branding of this chapter.

How Branding Works

Branding involves a set of marketing communication to distinguish a brand name or product from the competition. It is about creating a company identity, its product and activities and to make the market readily recognize it as such anywhere they are present. When you hear the name Coca-Cola you know it's a soda producing brand and Nike tells you it's a sporting shoe brand, of course, Apple will, and Calvin Klein will vividly describe the brand and what they do.

Therefore, branding works by using various marketing communication (including logo, trademark, brand loyalty, brand awareness, and brand management) strategies to distinguish a brand name from the competition. The primary goal of branding is to create customer loyalty through product differentiation and identity building to make the customer choose the brand product instead of that of the competition.

Branding Elements

Before you can successfully implement a branding strategy, you need the ingredients of branding called brand elements. These are the nut and bolts of banding that a branding expert needs to develop and execute a successful branding strategy; we identified 32 brand elements as follow:

1. Business Name

2. Logo

3. Colors

4. Tagline or Slogan

5. Fonts

6. Tone

7. Sounds

8. Smells

9. Business Cards

10. Emails

11. Workplace

12. Customer Service

13. Brand identity

14. Brand image

15. Brand positioning

16. Brand personality

17. Brand equity

18. Brand experience

19. Brand communication

20. Brand gap

21. Brand extension

22. Brand story

23. Brand differentiators

24. Brand promise

25. Theme Line

26. Shape

27. Graphics

28. Color

29. Sound

30. Movement

31. Taste

32. Website

A combination of these brand elements is used according to the brand expert to deliver a successful brand strategy that works.

Building a Brand Identity

Your brand is the perception of the market, and the process of doing that is through branding which involves the bringing together of carefully selected brand elements to make a meaningful combination to create a brand identity. Therefore, brand identity is the effect of the combination of a brand element that builds market perception. While branding aims to shape the market's opinion of your business, its product and general identity, brand perception is the process of achieving brand identity.

To build a brand identity requires that you know who you are and how you want to be seen by your market. To define who you are involved defining the following elements:

1. Your mission

2. Your values

3. Your brand personality

4. Unique selling proposition

5. Brand voice

To build a brand identity, here are 5 things to do:

1. Conduct an in-depth brand audit

2. Create your brand unique value proposition and brand statements

3. Create your brand creative elements

4. Execute your brand strategies to develop the brand identity

5. Evaluate and refine your brand identity

Brand Voice and Visuals

The critical elements in branding is the use of voice and visual identity to convey a brand message that sticks with the market for a long time. Branding uses the relevant channels of engagement with the audience (sight and sound) to develop a strong attachment to a brand. The idea of using voice and visual communication is to create a repetition of brand message. Using the logo, graphics, photo, color, and video to establish a visual connection and supported by voice message such as brand statement, slogan, brand promise, etc., to let the market take in a good dose of the branding message to establish a connection with the brand to drive loyalty.

Establishing a visual identity involves use of text typeface (font), brand theme, logo and color scheme, and style in a consistent manner to etch the fact in the mental mind of the audience. As with a brand voice, achieving cohesion is essential to create consistency in the brand message to allow it stick favorably with the audience. In other words, there should be a harmony of the visuals and voices in an engaging manner to build brand consciousness in the audience.

Finding your visual voice is vital in branding because this is the way to gainfully engage your audience in building trust, and loyalty for patronage of your brand offering. Think of a famous brand like Coca-Cola, the text, color and image used have been consistent over time across the world. At the same time, the voice that goes with the picture is same anywhere you go such that when you are in faraway places in the unfamiliar land, the brand makes it appears you are in your neighborhood.

Brand Applications

After all, said and done, the final stop of all branding activities is a brand application where every strategy is implemented in physical representation and consistent manner. You will often see the website, business cards, and monogram shirts, verbal and visual media including jingles signage, sponsored TV shows, uniforms, outdoor and interior design and branded merchandise and souvenirs.

Brand applications help to create a lasting and favorable impression and building market interest and support for the brand. Part of the communication brand applications will include brochures, posters, bulletins, video, magazine, and websites are all part of the grand branding design to give your business a lasting stake in the market.

What do you Want with Branding?

Branding offers you the opportunity to tell your story the way you want your audience or market to see you. Every element you employ in branding is aimed at communicating with the market from your perspective. It is a kind of you imposing what you want on the market using subtle means to drive home your point. You cannot afford to allow someone else to tell your story for you. If you leave a gap in your brand, I am sure someone will fill it, and the filling is probably not what you want the market to know about you.

It is unfortunate that majority of small businesses think branding is only for the big companies. This wrong perception has hindered many small businesses from growing, and it must change if you are to measure up with the ever-increasing competition in a world where there is a thin line between big and small businesses in term of struggling for what the market has to offer due to increase in global competition.

In closing, knowledge without application is a waste of time. I want to urge you as a business owner or manager to put this short intro to practice and begin the implementation of your branding now.

MARKETING IS JUST LIKE PLANTING A GARDEN

I remember growing up as a child and working in the garden with my grandmother. She was my sweetheart, and mentor. At the time, I did not realize how gifted and smart she was; I would sit in the garden and watch her dig the dirt and put the seed in to grow watermelons, collards, cabbages, potatoes', cucumbers, squash, and so much more. At first and for some–time there was no sign that anything was happening within the soil, and you could easily forget that something was.

My grandmother would go into the garden several days during the week, and she would pull the weeds, and water the garden. She'd need to keep the pests out too; she would have to tend to it. And then weeks later – I could see the fruit and vegetables grow! What I am saying is this, your business is much the same as gardening.

Now before you can do anything within a garden, you have to first have a vision of a garden and then you will need to actually create a garden. You need to break–ground and prepare.

You will need tools and knowledge, advice and eventually, physical effort.

First, you will need to decide what it is you are going to plant, and is it the right season for it; even to the extent of – is it the right location and climate? Good luck trying to grow bananas' in the cold climate.

As it is in gardening, so it is in business. You will have to have a right marketing plan, and branding. You will need to do some research and come up with some strategies; find out who your target market is and if the unique business will be sustainable in your area.

Can you see it? Have you planned how you are going to go about creating it? Will you have the right know–how to grow it, and create an abundant harvest? Don't lose sight of what's happening within your soil; especially when times get hard. It often seems fruitless, to start with when creating a new business. Think of this time as an opportunity to test different things and try new systems, products or processes. Think of it as a time to fine–tune your crop and do a bit of grafting to get the mix just right.

Next, when you have broken-ground and you have all the tools, people and wisdom to continue, then you will need to keep it in good condition and attract the right people to spend time and money in your garden. You will need to analyze your business–garden regularly. Promote some plants, and fertilize them, perhaps pull some plants out, to make way for other plants. Some of those plant could even be your staff . . . Oops, that's not fair! Well it is, especially if your staff has their own agenda, or they're not getting on board with your vision. This is your garden and you want it to be a success, don't you?

There is no point in growing it if it's just going to be neglected and waylaid. So be aware of pests and weeds that may try to creep into your business. These pests could be things like apathy, laziness, bad-attitudes, poor follow–up, and many others. It is a whole lot easier to create some-thing, than it is to maintain it, so keep your finger on the pulse. And just remember that gardens take time to grow; they don't happen overnight. There is a saying which I saw on the side of a freight truck once; it said . . . no one has ever been to the top of a mountain unless they have climbed it. This is so true. Don't expect to be at the summit of your business in a day, or a week, or even in a year! Good things, and things that are worth doing, take time.

NOW WHAT IS MARKETING?

Of course, this is not shopping! Though we often make this mistake in our daily life and go for marketing on special occasions like Xmas and like that. Marketing literally means "communicating the value of a product, service or brand to customers, for the purpose of promoting or selling that product, service, or brand". So, it is some kind of strategic attempt that you make sure to yield substantial business results. In short it is theme (the abstract part!) I am going to transform into real time benefits. Remember marketing is very simple. Even if I do not have the product or service readily available at hand, I can start marketing of the same. And this is what all the business promotion ads are doing round the clock.

How to do Marketing?

When I am baking a cake, I must follow certain recipes. Of course, I can make variations with flavors etc. but the main recipe remains unchanged. This is also valid for making gardens. I can make raised beds, flat beds and many more but must follow certain steps to have the flowers bloom. Marketing is as simple as that. Just plan including the expected challenges, analysis of the situation from all possible angles and having an alternative plan ready in case the first one fails to yield the desired results.

The Bottom Line

As I told earlier; marketing means creating permanent opportunity for the product or services and therefore I put stress on building scope of selling rather than the selling itself at the first stage. I prefer that you stop talking about yourself but tell the audience something they do not know. Simply speak their language and you will find marketing as slicing through cakes.

DIGITAL MARKETING MADE SIMPLE

No business will survive without selling and selling starts and ends with making your product and service known to the prospective buyer. For you to talk to your audience it is best to go where they are located; this is the advantage of Digital Marketing to bring you one on one with the target market.

Therefore, this chapter explores the fundamentals of digital marketing and shed more light on it from the perspective of business people whether domicile online or offline. In today's business world, you cannot avoid the internet; you will have to use it whether as a service provider or buyer. You can't run away from doing business online!

In this discussion, we will touch on vital areas of Digital Marketing and explain how each area will impact your business in significant ways. The importance of this chapter is to brace up to the challenges of modern techniques of interacting with your market to keep afloat and succeed in your business.

Topics to Cover

1. Introduction to Digital Marketing

2. 5 Reasons to use Digital Marketing Strategy in your business

3. Various parts of Digital Marketing

4. Making Digital Marketing work for you

5. Going greater heights with Digital Marketing

We intend for this to be a practical guide to Digital Marketing for business people, and entrepreneurs and it is going to be hands-on to reshape your perception of the subject matter.

Introduction to Digital Marketing

Digital marketing is the use of various online tools and resources to reach and engage with the prospective market to make them paying customers. Think of traditional marketing where you will go a great length to meet your target audience, so you can sell them what you have. The digital version of doing that in more efficient ways is known as digital marketing, and it presents a great potential as it breaks all restrictions of traditional marketing methods including national boundaries to give you access to nationals of other countries without being physically there.

5 Reasons to use Digital Marketing

Strategy in your Business

1. Ability to track your business progress

2. Global business opportunities

3. Lower cost of reaching your target market

4. Amazing free templates to manage your marketing strategy

5. Access to your ideal customers with insight into their heart desires

Various Parts of Digital Marketing

We talk about digital marketing being the use of different online tools and resources to reach and engage with prospective marketing; these are the various parts that make up digital marketing practice.

These include:

- Search Engine Optimization (SEO)

- SMS & Mobile Marketing

- Social Media Marketing

- Blogging & Content Marketing

- Web Analytics

- Branding and Online Advertisement

- Search Engine Marketing

- Conversion Optimization

- Sales funnel and Landing Page creation

- Infographics

- Vlogging & Video Marketing

As smart business minder, you need to understand all the tools and re-sources that make up digital marketing, so you can efficiently tap into the enormous potentials these business tools have for you. While it is possi-ble to outsource the delivery of any of these tools to a service provider, it would be more beneficial to understand what benefit each one holds for your business and be able to hire the best hands to help implement them.

Making Digital Marketing work for you

Digital marketing addresses the mechanisms of communicating with your audience to convert them into paying customers. It involves the use of wide-ranging strategies to boost consumer awareness of your prod-uct and services and give them cogent reasons to buy. Digital marketing strategy is a series of actions to help you achieve your marketing goal online. Therefore, your success in bringing each element of Digital mar-keting into a harmonious working relationship to build staying and loyal customer is the hallmark of digital marketing strategy.

To make digital marketing work for you, it needs knowledge, self-believe in the system and prompt action to stay on top of your game, always. It requires using the right technology and paying careful attention to the character of the audience you are trying to reach.

When implementing digital marketing, you need to be careful not to burn your resources on less efficient strategies. Where necessary, you need a combination of strategies to achieve a defined purpose.

Developing Digital Marketing Strategy Takes 5 Necessary Steps as Listed Below:

1. Define and understand what you want to achieve (objective setting): this involves knowing your business goal and pinpoint, accurately, what is essential and the achievement of which would move your business closer to its overall objectives. You need to set measurable goals and know how to measure your KPI (Key Performance Indicator) to see when you are there. The tools to use for this purpose include Google Analytics or use BuzzSumo, the tool to use is one that meets your business needs.

2. Learn from your past (every business makes a mistake, what is yours?): The reality of the past is a factor in planning an effective digital marketing strategy for the future. Take time to understand how you got here and planned how to move to your target destination in business. If you are starting a new business, it is best to set up your analytics to capture every moment of your business activity so that going back in the future with facts and figure will be easier for you. At every milestone in your business, pause to ask vital questions that will open the way to make landmark discovery and breakthrough. Some tools you can use include Google's benchmarking Reports and SEMrush to sniff on competition activity.

3. Resonate with your audience (speak the language your market understands): the social audience has unique characteristics and

the style of communication that best appeal to them, an efficient digital marketing strategy should hinge on talking to your audience in their language so that you will get maximum affirmative and succeed with more conversions. How much your audience respond to your advances determine your success; social marketing is about engagement, and that is the way to know what your audience needs. A module found in Google Analytics is Audience Reports that help to identify your audience key features including their persona, sex, career, age and other to help you plan efficiently for their needs.

4. Know your means (Know how much and plan what you can afford): You need to have three things to identify this. They include budget, channels, and people. These three means identifying elements help you to successfully implement the right digital marketing strategy without falling short on vital resources. Every marketing plan needs to have a cost to it, you need to know the various marketing channels to deploy for your marketing plan, and finally, the two resources will be under the management of your human resource. Once you know your means and can handle it efficiently, you are success bound!

5. Be dynamic (nothing is permanent): Having gone through the four-marketing strategy building steps above, you should know that nothing ever comes out perfect at the onset. Treat your strategy as work in progress to identify downside early and fix it. This will be continuous until you have successfully achieved your goal. For a successful digital marketing strategy, you need to know your starting and end and install an efficient monitoring system to follow up on your marketing practice.

Going Greater Heights with Digital Marketing

Now that you know a bit about digital marketing, you should understand that it is a continuous learning procedure because the internet world improves every day and the dynamism of digital marketing is changing and getting better with improvement in technology. As you sharpen your business goals and objectives, it is essential you communicate these to your target audience in the most understandable manner.

Because you ran a successful digital marketing campaign last year does not mean the same strategy would work again this year. As you set new challenges, define your audience and come up with the best online marketing strategy that will deliver the best results.

TRADITIONAL MARKETING VERSUS SOCIAL MEDIA MARKETING

We all talk about marketing. But what is marketing? In simple terms it is the process of communicating the value of a product or services to potential users with an intention to promote or increasing sales of the product or services. Understanding traditional and social media marketing becomes easier if we correlate these to our CD or DVD selection process. What we do when we enter a kiosk lending those for viewing at home. After brooding over for some time on series of the CDs and DVDs stock most of us ultimately select the CD we heard someone has viewed. But why it is so? The simple answer is that we do not trust what is printed on the CDs but count on referrals.

The virtual world

Present era is the era of communication when people are using internet and different apps for sharing and viewing information. This new way of communication has such an impact that the internet is now loaded with all sorts of information one may desire to have. Every moment millions of people are assessing the net and such user density made it as a tool of creating opportunity.

What is traditional marketing?

Traditional marketing is mainly advertisement based and dates to the Egyptian civilization when papyrus was used for making wall posters. It is the much-recognized type of marketing that are categorized as using print media for advertising the product or services, on air broadcasting through radio & television, direct mailing such as sending brochures and making telephone calls.

IMPORTANCE OF RIGHT MARKETING STRATEGY

Marketing strategies are essential to promote a brand and to increase its use resulting tangible financial advantage. It includes many business activities including market analysis, launching of the products and targeting the potential customers. The business owners and executives therefore need to know the importance of the right marketing strategies for building target markets efficiently. These are always a part of the brainstorming process and include the price of the product or services, its distribution or implementation for making substantial changes in the bottom line of the business. There is nothing right or wrong in marketing. No rigid market strategy can bring success. Your strategy should be totally changed or amended based on the change in market and customer profile.

How to choose the right strategy?

It all depends on the group of your potential customers. If your brand is meant for the use of the busy executives, it is always preferable to go online and specially take the help of web contents because this can convey the right message to them in short time through displays.

For targeting the younger generation any or all of three will suffice, though advertising through visuals always attract the customer best. And for the retired, offline written content yields better results as this segment of potential customers always prefer to read hard copies rather than searching webs.

VIRTUAL MARKETING

We all know that "ill news runs apace". But have we ever thought why it is like that? Let us look at the adage again. The inner meaning of this adage is that not all news runs apace. There are two words 'ill' and 'apace'. These two words are the cardinal points of viral marketing. The first word 'ill' is the cause and the second word 'apace' is the effect. Now if I ask why it runs apace; the prompt reply would be that it is ill. But what this is about? It means that anything to have probability to run apace must trigger emotions. So is the case of viral marketing. It must be able to trigger emotions of the viewers to run apace which in internet marketing is to be viral.

What it is?

It refers to marketing techniques that produces exponential increase in brand awareness or attain other marketing goals. This is a self-replicating process analogue to the spread of viruses. While the simplest viral marketing was like spreading rumors by whispering campaign, on the realm of internet, it stands for the marketing techniques that influence the websites and/or the users to pass on specific marketing information to other sites and/or users for enhancing the visibility and effect of the message. In such strategies of marketing the message appeal to individuals with high social networking potential or SNP for further transmissions to reach a great number of audience in a very short period of time.

How does it work?

As amoebas can grow in numbers by cell division, viruses can also replicate themselves continuously in doubling the number in each generation as on next page.

O

OO

OOOO

OOOOOOO

OOOOOOOOOOOOOOOO

OOOOOOOOOOOOOOOOOOOOOOOOOOOOOOOOO

And their population surpasses all imaginations in very few generations!

Basing on this viral marketing involves communicating marketing messages to others creating opportunities for growth by attracting prospecting viewers. When carefully planned this yield very good results.

How to create a viral campaign?

Though each marketer wants the campaign to go viral, it is impossible to predict which will go viral and which will flounder. However, following these basic steps can increase the probability of the campaign going viral.

- Making it visually appealing: Even if the message is primarily text based, a compelling video must be added that matches the product or services.

- Planning the campaign: Most of the successful viral marketing campaign is carefully planned. The campaign should include a good iconographic for clear communication of the message.

- Tickling emotions: To go viral the campaign should tug on emotions of the viewers and as such they must be designed with emotional catches.

- Knowing the audience: The campaigner must have clear ideas about the target audience and the emotional triggers required to awaken them. Moreover, it is also important to know when they are most likely to be online visiting social sites and launching the campaign at the appropriate hour.

- Making it simple and casual: Never try to force anything on the viewers. They have their own sense of judgment and therefore your campaign should be simple and with a carefully planned casual approach.

SWOT ANALYSIS

When staying alone I had to manage all my daily chores from cooking to cleaning. You won't believe that it took me several eggs to learn just how to boil eggs perfectly. In the first attempt the eggs were less than half boiled and next time I let it boil more ending with an almost dry pan and the egg with cracked shells was somewhere between boiled and burnt egg. After tracking back, the process followed in my mind I found that I have ignored certain basic principles. I have employed all my strengths like applying heat for boiling water but did not consider the fact that boiling for long hours will evaporate the water. Then I started looking for alternatives and after thinking for another couple of minutes I adjusted water and heat with constant vigil and eventually got a boiled egg for my breakfast. Later that day I concluded that if I have planned the process considering the helpful and harmful elements, then in all probabilities I would have been successful in the first attempt.

What is SWOT?

It is the abbreviation of STRENGTHS, WEAKNESSES, OPPORTU-NITIES & THREATS.

SWOT planning is a structured process of planning that takes care of all these four elements in any process for achieving desired results. Out of these four elements Strengths and Opportunities are helpful elements for achieving the objective and weaknesses and threats are the harmful elements hindering achievement.

How it can help?

SWOT requires nothing but a little thought. If done properly it has the power to uncover hidden opportunities for exploitation and when the weaknesses are clearly understood it makes you alert and you can eliminate the threats. This simple technique is equally applicable in all processes and when applied in the context of business projects, it helps to have an edge over the competitors due to its inherent property to reduce failures. It can be used as a starting kit and as strategic tool in making business decisions. In fact, for my every planning of personal and business projects I resort to SWOT analysis.

SWOT is a kind of self-analysis. It is best done by preparing a checklist containing questions on all the four elements of SWOT. These questions should be answered to generate meaningful information and brainstorming must be done to do SWOT analysis.

How to use it?

There is again a crux. In any business process the Strengths and Weaknesses are often your internal factors or the hard realities and the Opportunities and Threats, the abstract ones, are mostly due to the external factors. In every business you must see how both the internal and external environments match.

Opportunities may also arise from new technologies, further investments and the state policies. It is; therefore, always better to analyze the strengths and elements for achieving best performance. A good way to look at the opportunities is to revisit the strengths and weaknesses. You must try to find out if the strengths open up any opportunity and how you can create new opportunities by reducing, if not totally eliminating, your weaknesses.

And when you do this it will make you ready for eliminating threats. I would suggest that, after you are familiar with SWOT, you should try the TOWS analysis, in the reverse direction, treating external elements first.

TARGET MARKET

Learn how to reach your target market and niche to gain more consumers.

Creating a perfect marketing tool for reaching the target market and gaining more customers is not easy. It varies from organization to organization depending on the realities they are banking upon and the abstracts they want to achieve. Even a small business can create very strong and meaningful marketing strategy based on their specific conditions.

Let me tell you the story of a Japanese company that made the traditional Japanese screens for decorating and dividing rooms. As there were more and more modern apartments for contemporary living styles, there was an obvious recess in the market of the company. Do you know what they do? At the next trade show they recreated their workshop there and brought their traditional artisans who have spent their lives making ornamental screens to the trade show stall. The artisans started making screens in the stalls. At first nothing happened, but after some time crowed started to gather to watch the astounding intricacy and fascinating craftsmanship of the product. They did not brag or advocated their product, but the silent show helped them to revive.

This strategy helped them and so you can make your own strategy to reach the target market depending on your exact condition.

WHAT IS A TARGET MARKET?

The target market means a specific cluster of customers that a business aim and evolve its marketing efforts around the group and finally sell their product or services to this cluster of customers.

How to define and reach the target market?

Even before you plan to launch any marketing campaign, you must know the target market. That is who will buy your product or services, how to appeal and persuade them. The following steps will help you in defining and reaching your target market easily.

- Defining the target market: As a gardener clear the weeds from the garden, you should also discard the 'maybes' first for keeping your marketing campaign focused and at the same time cost effective. It is better to stratify the target market based on demographics that is their personal details like profession, income etc. psychographics or their attitudes, values, likings etc. And behavior including their consuming habits.

- Reaching the target market: Once you are sure about the target market, you must find ways to reach them and

the basic principle about this is 'fish where it is available'. If your target market consists of busy professionals of 25 to 35 years, you should try engaging them through social media and online activities. On the other hand, if your target market is made of mostly retired people of 55 to 65 years, it is better to opt for printed materials as they love to read. Whatever line you may follow, you must ask the advertising managers to analyze profiles for effective marketing.

- Identifying the types: There many customers who always switch brands influenced by promotional offers. So, you must be aware of the customers i.e. if they are your existing ones or new or the switching type to set your campaign accordingly.

• Customizing strategy: As you have the knowledge of the customers you must follow the appropriate method to reach, engage and for gaining new customers.

IMPORTANCE OF WRITTEN CONTENT

Whether you believe or not we all are addicted to stories. Even when the body sleeps the mind stays awake telling stories about many things. Stories are great way for conveying messages even in the field of marketing too. Let me tell you a story about strategy.

There was a man in old days; very naive and simple, always speaking from his heart. Once he was travelling to the capital for searching jobs. It was dark when he reached the capital. Knowing not where to stay, he knocked the door of the first house. Someone from inside enquired what did he want. He said that he wanted a place to sleep. Prompt came the harsh reply "Not possible. There are ladies." So, he knocked the door of another house. And when someone asked who it was, he enquired if there were ladies inside. Prompt opened the door and the householder asked, "Why"? The man replied I would like to sleep. You all can guess what happened next. Marketing is like that only. You can never except that the same thing will work at all always.

Before we dig further let us have a curtain raiser on web copy, web content and written content.

Web Copy, Web Content, Written Content

Web copies are SEO friendly, short and best for sharing. These contain product description and inspirational thought about the product or services

Web contents comprise of aural, textual, visual contents encountered as a part of the user experience on websites. It may, among other things, include any or all of images, sounds, videos and animations.

Written content contains only textual description of the product or services intended to be promoted and usually published offline, through online written contents are also in use.

VISION, MISSION, & VALUES STATEMENTS

None of us can deny that messages are better conveyed through stories than hundred words. If I say "We must build a great organization for unleashing the creativity and focusing the corporate activities that will enable to develop the most efficient product or services in world. To offer our customers only the best and cost-effective product or service with our state-of-the technology that will be energy efficient and environment friendly" and ask anyone to repeat it, I do not know if anyone would be able to tell. This is because it does not put a print on our mind and, therefore, how much informative it maybe we really do not recognize the meaning and naturally will not be able to follow. Most of the vision, mission and values stamens are like that. Those stay there hanged but being purely ornamental is hardly of any help.

What are those then?

- Vision statements contain the objective of the organization based on economic considerations and are intended to provide guidance on decision making. A carefully crafted vision statement helps to communicate goals to employees throughout the organization.

- Mission statements convey the purpose of the organization and serve as filters to separate important from the unimportant ones focusing on the status, the activities and the purposes.

- Value statements inform the customers and the employees of an organization about the priorities and beliefs of the organization. These are used also for connecting the target customers.

Understanding Vision, Mission & Value Statements

Quite often these two are jumbled up though they are distinctly different. So, how to understand the difference? Let me tell you the best way to understand these clearly. To do this let us add 'ARY' to both words and see what happens.

Vision + ARY = Visionary

Mission + ARY = Missionary

So, these two coined words now seem to be quite familiar as we know what these people do in the society. Visionary is someone who can see the potential of something like Jesus Christ who knew what was possible. The value statements describe the fundamental principles creating positive image of the organization.

How to write these?

There is no point in putting all the good words together as the example I cited earlier. These are like twitters and never help to achieve objectives. The vision, mission and values statements should be crafted in simple language making the future, stating what is possible and defining how it will be done.

ADVERTISING

Do you want to become a successful business person, with a thriving business? Then you will need to invest in your business. This is a no–brainer, for instance you will need to throw in a budget for advertising if you are to reach a wider target audience. Advertising can be a burden, but it is an essential part of the process. Regular advertising works better than something every now and then. People only actively see advertising when they're looking for something, or if something catches their eye; so, you may feel it's not really working sometimes. But regular promoting will bring you and your business to the forefront of someone's mind when they're ready, and in the market for something.

A fantastic way to advertise is to get involved with local groups of business professionals, regularly, even weekly. Groups such as BNI, (Business Network International) are fantastic! The business people that attend these groups effectively become your eyes and ears on the ground for you, and your business. They pass on qualified referrals to you, and you will tend do the same for them. The philosophy behind it is called givers gain. Besides, advertising can usually be 100% reclaimable when the tax man comes–a– knocking.

You may have to hire staff to help run the business (hopefully you will need to, and many of them!). If you are trying to produce too much beyond your individual capabilities and enterprise and trying to do everything yourself, this could create bad customer service, and an unprofessional business result; you will effectively hamstring your business.

Don't be afraid of increase; in fact, reach for it. Some people hinder their own progress because they fear failure. If for example, you're a painter and you see advertised a large-scale contract; we'll, do the numbers, put in your tender and get it! But make sure you cover all your bases, hire the staff you will need, and get that extra equipment you're going to have to have and then do the right thing: get stuck into it with gusto and professionalism. And, most importantly, produce quality results. If you don't, then that's going to really reflect badly on any prospects.

Synergy is a powerful force; for example, one Clydesdale horse can pull about 2 ton, but two Clydesdale horses' together, can pull 8 tons'! Having staff on board, will drive you harder, and you will achieve much more. And if you achieve much more, than you can receive much more.

SUCCESSFUL STEPS TO EVENT PLANNING

When in this present age of Instagram, Twitter, Face book, LinkedIn and when we can also share information using VoIP and webinars what could be the utility of holding customer events? Though the idea of holding events may seem to be outdated in the virtual world of communication; holding events is still a very strong way for improving customer relation and for creating a buzz in the market.

I have specialization in event planning & event marketing and I enjoy doing it. Through my long exposure in this field, at last I learned that you require detailed planning and tight execution for making an event success.

Before I start dwelling on the stepping stones of event planning let us share a few words about events and their benefits.

Events and their benefits

Event can mean anything from social gathering, wedding ceremonies, school formals, festivities, conferences and many more. But for the purpose of marketing we shall confine our discussions on understanding a brand identifying target audiences, detailing the logistics and others for launching customer events.

Managing events is used as marketing tools by many organizations, big and small. Events may also include elements like music & entertainment or specially chosen venue to influence the theme of the event.

How much you may communicate with your customers and clients in the virtual world, personal interaction has unique advantage of creating brand loyalty, generating referrals and increasing sales as well. These help to have direct interaction with the industry populace for sharing innovative ideas, opportunities and partnership.

The stepping stones

Like any other thing in your life events also require great amount of detailed planning involving the following steps.

1. Developing the goal & objective: You should be clear in mind why you are going to hold the event and what you expect to achieve out of it.

2. Assessing the resources and constraints: You should assess all your resources like the peers, staff members, community groups besides financial resources and must also identify the areas of hindrances.

3. Organizing the team: Events require concerted efforts and therefore you must form a team with members having experience in different aspects under the Event Manager. Members of the team should have allocated responsibilities of different functions like venue management, publicity management, sponsoring arrangement etc.

4. Brainstorming ideas: If you desire to have a unique event you must do sufficient brain storming on the theme and its implementation. All ideas must be accepted with equal importance to get the best out of those.

5. Setting the date: This is very vital as nothing succeeds without a target. But you must allow enough time for smooth implementation and check with the speakers and participants about their availability to make it a grand success.

6. Branding the event: Events should be branded with catching theme for success.

7. Developing budget: Consider all associated costs and sponsoring amounts for forming a realistic budget.

8. Creating Master Plan: These should include all administrative process of managing venue, registration, speakers, publicity & promotion, follow up dinners etc.

9. Identifying partners and sponsors: This includes finding corporate and community patronization for funds and organizing venues.

10. Structuring evaluation process: You must form tools to scaling the success of the events and the impact it created.

EXPERIENTIAL MARKETING

When thinking of marketing, the average person will think of TV commercials, flyers, and radio commercials. The objective being to describe the benefits, features and characteristics, however a new approach to marketing allows for consumers experience the brand or product directly, creating a special bond. While many use experiential marketing in parallel with their traditional marketing campaigns, only some combinations have shown excellent results. Experiential marketing is most common in the form of an event, where it gives the company the opportunity to form long term connections with future clients.

Experiential marketing is often referred to as 'Event marketing' and is primarily because there is no better way to form a special connection between consumer and brand than in person at an event. While traditional marketing methods introduce a product and provide an idea of what a brand or product is like, event marketing allows the brand to create a special bond, which in turn creates loyalty and influence. Events come in several forms, each of which have their own benefits. Some examples include conventions, fundraisers, conferences, workshops, exhibitions, fairs, and much more. Grand Openings, for example, is an excellent way to start forming connections from the get go. They are commonly planned for new restaurants, as well as other establishments.

Planning these events require a high level of expertise and understanding of event marketing, and with the proper event planning, it can jumpstart a new business, or even revitalize a dying one.

NETWORKING AND REFERRAL

I do not know how many of you have seen fishermen fishing with nets. When I first saw it in my childhood, I was simply taken aback seeing those getting fishes from under the water. But when I think of the same process at this grown age, it teaches me many things about network and referrals. But how? It is simple. Just try to trace back what the fishermen do step by step. They get their net – choose a spot – cast the net and after a while start pulling it out. The results: they find number fishes in the net.

As the fishes are stored, they repeat the process severally for more catches having idea of their daily requirement. Have you noticed any specialty of the process? Let me tell you that the fishermen never concentrate on the individual fishes as they can never guess what fish will be caught in the net but remain solely concerned over casting of the net.

Marketing through networking and referrals is same as fishing with a net. Like the fishermen who never have the idea of the size of the fish beforehand but knows that once caught it belongs to him and therefore focuses on casting only. Networking and referrals also give you no preconceived idea of your prospecting client but ensures that when someone comes, you can keep him loyal to your brand for business growth profitability.

What is networking and referral?

Networking is literally a socio-commercial activity that helps people to recognize, create and take actions on business opportunities. And by referral we mean business promotion through third-party introduction. The primitive form of referral is the word of mouth and you can influence networking and referral for sustainable business returns by applying appropriate strategies.

Many of us have the misconception that the referrals obtained are due to chance factor only and have no connection whatsoever with gaining new clients. Believe me, for networking and referral, what you say luck or chance factor is simply persistence finding opportunities. As such there should be continuous networking and referral activities for business prosperity.

Why networking and referral work?

Networking and referral are the natural outcome of everyday business activities. Though at the beginning it looks like to be chaotic, but this works well at the end. It works because of the reward the customer or the visitors get in return of referring people to your network. Suppose 'A' buys something from you, he gets a referral link for inviting others to your stores. Next 'B' receives email from 'A' with his referral link and buys from your stores and the cycle is repeated.

How to build referrals?

Third party endorsement is the most powerful vehicle for successful marketing. In every business many clienteles comes through referrals. Following tips will help to build a solid referral program.

- Identifying sources

- Adopting long-term approach

- Understanding the requirements and motives Creating a business group

- Taking care of the referral sources.

The Final Words

Networking and referral is the right step to keep growing as it saves time, enhance relationship and reduce marketing costs.

COLLABORATION AND PARTNERSHIP

We are stronger in numbers: collaboration and partnership

I think most of us are aware of the adage "United we stand divided we fall". But if asked to use this policy in their business activities, they fail miserably. Being stuck up with the age-old hypothesis of competition they ignore the role of companionship as a great tool for achieving their goals.

Why collaboration is the key to successful marketing?

None can deny that there is strength in numbers. Brand partnership works through the loan of the brand equity. Brand collaboration helps to satisfy a period of time and function. Thus, collaboration is not mere a strategy but the vital key for winning marketing battles for long term business growth.

Power of Collaboration and Partnership

Collaboration and partnership helps to overcome business challenges. It increases business effectiveness through joint marketing activities. It also helps to widen the marketing reach and utilizes the expertise of the professionals for group benefit. Further it works towards building of mutual trust and brings relevance, enhances creativity & resources for co-branding activities unveiling the hidden opportunities and decreasing the individual cost of marketing.

Collaboration and partnership also help to arrive at the best solution in least possible time.

How does it work?

Having a brand partner is something like introducing your favorite 'X' to your pub mates. When you do so, you are unconsciously using endorsement options to get 'X' to reach new audiences. As you further engage with the group of your brand partner, the group becomes two times larger and naturally your marketing efforts and their effects also get doubled. It may also grow further depending on the effort of the group.

Setting Marketing Collaboration

Finding new customers is a challenging job every business face. Setting up strategic partnership for marketing is a cost-effective way to reach new audiences. The process of collaboration and partnership begins with identifying the goal. To be successful one also must wear the customer shoes i.e. think like a customer. What are the brands the customers are interacting now? What they are aspiring for? And all such questions need to be answered from a customer point of view. Once this is done the next step is to focus on the relationship to make things happen favorably with a clear but flexible planning to achieve common goal. By amplifying partnership, one can get better ROI.

Who to collaborate with?

This is very pertinent question and is apt rise in your minds. You can identify partners either through contacts or through networking. One can also take the help of experts who can align thoughts, agendas and expectations and once a prospective partner is found consider your mission, corporate social responsibility and identity for forming a strategic marketing collaboration.

RUN YOUR OWN RACE

Have you ever looked at someone else's business and thought, I could do that, and I could do it better? You probably could, but should you? Competition is good sure, but it can also take you away from the real deal . . . the people you are dealing with and the clientele that are familiar with you and what you offer! Now I'm not promoting that you should bow to everyone's expectations, far from it. No, I'm suggesting that, perhaps that business which you're looking at and thinking, I could do better, is already covering the need and there is in fact another need for you to fulfil.

Run your race; use your skills and abilities. Because if you try to be someone else than you will only ever be a second rate someone else. Be the best that you can be and be the best at being you.

So many business owners try to keep up with other business owners and become distracted. Their focus is on their competitors, or business owners they're trying to beat, and not their own clients! Look out for your competition and even bounce off their promotions etc. Go so far as to even show your customers what they offer, and what you have, and why you have the better deal and benefits as it were. To be armed with the competitors' ammunition is a power indeed. This shows that you are up to the plate and know your stuff. This gives your clients confidence in who you are, what you stand for, and can even sew a little seed of doubt as to what your opposition may or may not have or do.

"Don't get distracted by competing with others. Run your race. You have exactly what you need for your assignment. Learn to accept your gifts." said Joel Osteen, a prominent minister of our hour. And by accepting your gifts and talents, you will have the upper hand; you will do well, and you will not appear false in any way. Because people can easily see through pretenses; and you don't want to be someone not to be trusted. Trust goes a long way in securing business and creating repeat clientele. This is something we all can appreciate.

STAY RELEVANT

As a business owner, you should always keep up with the current trends in your business genre and the competitions; constantly promoting yourself.

At times you may need to collaborate and partner up with others and use their unique skills and attributes to help yourself with staying relevant. Celebrities do this all the time. For instance, many singers promote themselves by singing something of their own or someone else's with a hot and current celebrity, and by doing so, they are staying relevant: re-connecting with the masses. A great example is Dancing with the Stars, and Celebrity Apprentice. Many stars we have not seen on the scene for years, suddenly start appearing on these shows. By doing this they obtain a lot of press, and many even get hired for commercials, or sitcoms. At times you have to reinvent yourself to up your game.

It's not too difficult to do, you just need to come up with an idea and take some risks with it. Try having a brainstorming session with like–minded individuals; think outside the square. Write some things down and expand on them.

I know of a person who had been involved with theatre on a few occasions, doing shows and dramas, and even appearing on television commercials once or twice. Then life suddenly got too busy, and they had to pull away from their passion, and get onto the straight and narrow; raising kids and being a family man, working a normal 9–5 job etc. Not an uncommon story. But he still had the passion smoldering away inside, and it wasn't getting used; instead it almost became dead, which was a real shame. These things do happen; you may have had a successful business and were going for it, being successful, fulfilled and prospering. And then suddenly it's not happening so much; sales may be down, ideas may be lean: dwindling.

It's times like these that you need to get help and advice from those that are doing well and are prospering in their own right. Don't copy them but do something with their advice. I'm sure they would gladly offer you help, so long as you're not a threat or a competitor to them; and so long as you reach out and ask.

So, what happened to this thespian that I mentioned earlier? Well, he reinvented himself. He looked at the skills he had, and a way to use them that wouldn't encroach on his new–found life and family. Now days you can find him writing those dramas he was once performing, and, he uses his acting skills to do something completely different to what he used to do. Now, he's using those skills for audiobooks, and voice acting. It sure takes up a whole lot less time than his previous, endless auditions, and production preparation of old. He looked outside the square and did something different. There's an old saying that goes something like this . . . if you keep doing the same things that you have always done, then you will always get the same results that you have always had. Look around, look outside your bubble and find a sparkle of difference. Then be pro-active and check it out. I'm sure you will surprise yourself.

STAY IN YOUR LANE

What I have observed over the years is this, business owners don't realize their focus should be running their own business; too many try to be the jack of all trades and only end up positioning themselves for failure. For instance, if you're not a graphic designer, don't try to be one as this will only hinder your branding. Sure, it's a good idea to learn about graphic design; but consult with the people who have their graphic design credentials down–pat.

Some business owners seek people who may be a business owner, and because they appear to be successful in their business, they obtain business advice from them. Business Owners should seek out people that have credential in the business industry if they wish to learn how to have a successful business.

If you're sick, would you go to a Doctor that has credentials, or go to one without them? It's the same with business; get involved with business professionals with credentials and experience. And let them be your guide. It's their niche; you concentrate on your niche. Stay in your lane.

If you need graphics, and you're are a novice graphic designer, hire a professional graphic designer; and learn from them. If you want your marketing material to look like the big boys, then you need professional graphics, not tacky graphics.

It's the same when it comes to photography for your business. Many people take pictures with their phones and wonder why the pictures don't come out–well, professional. Oh dear, some will even use those pictures for their branding and it will only make your business look very unprofessional. This is a trap to avoid.

I know people who have done just that, and unless you have trained eyes to see the errors, you will miss them completely. Try this little experiment and you will see what I mean . . . Imagine a brand of car; not one you're used to, but a different brand. For example, if you drive a Honda, you tend to see lots of other Hondas' on your way to work or town, or where–ever. But if you think about a European brand that you're not familiar with: say a Skoda, or a Mercedes. Do you ever see any of them? Probably not. Now pick one of these brands and then go for a drive just to see if you can find some. I'll bet you will see a whole lot more than you have ever seen before. Isn't that amazing?

Now why is that you may wonder? The fact is, those cars have always been there, only you didn't notice them until they became part of your world. But they have always been in the world of those that drive them. They will even be able to tell you that the indicator lights and the wiper switches are on the other side of the steering column.

My point is, you can have knowledge of things; photography, videography, graphic design etc., but to have wisdom about a product or service takes years to learn and master. Stay in your lane, and you will see the whole road ahead more clearly.

KNOW YOUR VALUE

When I first began providing marketing services, I did some work for free and bartered, offering my services to others in exchange for something of theirs. The reason why I chose to work that way at the time, was because I was in graduate school and then I went on to doctoral school. I helped many business owners grow, and have success with their planned events etc. The problem was, I wasn't making any monies myself; yet I worked tirelessly on their marketing campaigns', and branding; putting in all the effort, with no monetary returns.

Well it came to a point where I wanted to be compensated for my work with some financial substance, and why shouldn't I? Working for free is ok, for a time, and for certain reasons: but we should not camp there.

When I provided a price list of my services, and invoices I had not received payment for: I learned to value myself. Up until that point, I was an easy target for abuse of services because I did not value my expertise. Now this is not an unusual story, people do it all the time: and not always with intention. Sometimes others just don't really think about what you have done for them and made the connection that what you have done (and wonderfully) must've been a real sacrifice for you to carry out. So when you learn that what you have, is valuable, and that others will need it in some way; then don't be shy: put some monetary value upon it. People will not mind paying for your work, and they will certainly see that you do earn it.

Don't undermine yourself and your special, unique abilities. Some people will be upset about having to pay for something that they could have . . . once–upon–a–time, had for free; but if those people do not make the connection and value your work, then let them go; they will only end up being a hindrance to your progress anyway. The last thing you need is to be burning the candle at both ends, for nothing!

We must do an audit on ourselves from time to time, we need to put in writing some ballpark figures of what we are doing and what it should be worth. If you don't really know where to start, well then start with how much you would like to earn over the year. Divide that up by months and weeks, and finally hours. Ask yourself, how much should I charge per hour for my services? And don't forget to throw in the expenses after you've come up with that hourly rate, or you'll come up short.

Value your time, and what you produce with your time. Put your stake in the ground, and others will value that time too, and you. They will finally make the connection that, really you are helping them to achieve their goals: and as the old saying goes . . . success, breeds success. If they are achieving their goals, then you will too.

CHARACTER

A beaming character can make all the difference in marketing!

The legendary President of America, Abraham Lincoln, once said, "Reputation is the shadow; character is the tree." In fact, our character is much more than what we would presume.

Many people are talented and can woe the crowds with their abilities and feats, they can lead whole armies to a battlefield with their charisma and zeal. Talent can shoot people to stardom in quick succession, make them lots of money, and gain huge followings. But it's not people's talent that endures the fires– to–come, it's their character. Talent can take you anywhere, but it is only character that will (or will not) sustain you. When the overnight successes are opened for all to see, the cracks will surely show.

Some people do not have good character. I remember my Grandmother telling me, it's your actions that speak louder than your words. This is so true; this has stayed with me throughout my life. We ought to listen to our grandmothers.

What is a diamond? It is a small piece of carbon that has survived massive pressures, over a long period of time. What is a mighty oak tree? It's a small nut that has stood its ground. Character is the same . . . character is simply, who we are when

no one is looking. It's the core makeup of a person that sets them apart, and if your character has cracks, and if it's weak or has secret little issues, then they will only increase in size until eventually you simply fall apart.

Everyone in this world has character of some sort; we might say that Mr. X or Y does not have any character. Character may be considered as an evaluation of the inherent moral qualities of an individual. This includes qualities such as honesty, fortitude, empathy and many more. Character is determined by the existence of what we call virtues and the absence of the so called social vices. And before we come to any conclusions about the character of any individual, we must ensure the presence of good qualities, and the absence of bad qualities.

The fundamentals of character

- Trustworthiness: One should not deceive or betray anyone, be reliable always, must implement what has been said and moreover have the courage to do the right things and stand by everyone.

- Respect: One must follow the golden rule that there would always be differences and learn to respect the other views. All disagreements should be dealt with patience to arrive at the best solution based on mutual respect.

- Responsibility: One should not hesitate to do what he is supposed to do. Must plan and stick to the plan and always keep on trying.

- Accountability: One must set good examples being accountable for words, attitudes and deeds.

- Fairness: One must always be ethical, open minded and treat everyone fairly without blaming.

- Caring: One should also be compassionate & caring helping people in need and express gratitude to the helping friends.

- Citizenship: One must do his share for the benefit and betterment of the community and help to protect environment.

Character vs reputation

Character and reputation are distinctly different. While your reputation says what the people think about you, your character determines who you really are. Most of the people tend to believe what other makes them believe and thus enhance their fall. I can cite you hundreds of cases where the person involved was very reputed and worked seamlessly on the reputation but had terrible character. And when, through intimacy, the character became known, the person was completely ruined. So, it is always better to count on character rather than on reputation because basing on character means you are working on the stuff that is inherent in you and not imposed by others.

GOAL SETTING

You should set goals first for achieving success in everything.

Can anyone tell me what makes lives different? I know there will be hundreds of different stories. But when you summarize these, the basic reason comes out to be goal setting.

Let me tell you something about a business school. This is all about their student's achievements. They selected groups of students and evaluated them based on their grades and future plans. The college further evaluated them 10 years after they have passed and came out with surprising findings. The study revealed that the most successful were not the students who used to achieve higher grades, but those who had specific future plans even 10 years ago. So, there lies the difference between the successful and unsuccessful people. To be successful one must have a goal and know where they want to go for reaching their ultimately. Obviously, the next question will be how to achieve goals? Like to visit a place you must know that place first, to achieve goals in business, personal life or events one should know how to set those first.

Focusing: the great tool

Most of us are unaware of the power of focusing and never really focus. We have the typical habit to concentrate on many things simultaneously and thus loose our eye from what we actually want to achieve. If a plank is placed on the floor and ask you to walk on the plank from one end to the other all of you will certainly be able to do the same quite easily. But if I place a plank connecting the roofs of two tall buildings across the street, hardly one or two will be able to make it. This is because most of you will start on thinking what will happen you slip and from fall from such a great height and thus losing the focus on the entrusted job. After setting the goal you should concentrate on that only and must stay focused always or achieving the target.

What are goals?

A goal is the desired result that any individual or business organization plan and engage to achieve within a definite time frame or deadline. This should not be mixed with visions which are most of the times unspecific and not scalable like staying healthy. But a goal is an aim that can be measured. Further it should be achievable. If you set a goal of topping the Everest without having mountaineering training, it can be termed as your dream but not goal because it is not realistic.

What are short term & long-term goals?

Short term goals are the things that you want to do soon, may be a week, a month or a year, such as paying your credit card bills at the month end. These help you to focus on what you can do right away. Usually these are the parts of the larger targets and guide you towards achieving the long-term goal. On the other hand, long term goals are those you wish to achieve in the distant future. Usually these are the culmination of various short-term goals achieved in parts. While the short terms goals are like making your credit card payments on time, the long-term goal is to have good credit rating that will be helpful for securing further credits.

How to set goals?

You can best understand the short term and long-term goals and what they are all about by following the limited over cricket matches when a team chases a target score. As they lose several wickets, they set their target of runs for every over for ultimately winning the match.

Effective goal setting determines how an individual or business will succeed. There are six golden rules of goal setting as below:

1. Only set the goal that motivates you: The goal should be important and relate to the high priorities in life. It should be able to push you beyond your present level and must have some values in achieving.

2. Set realistic goals only: To do this you should follow the 'SMART' principle. That is your goal should be Specific, Measurable, Attainable, Relevant & Timed.

3. Put it in writing: When you write the goal, it becomes tangible and as you can see it always there is no way to forget the same. Moreover, when displayed it reminds you of the task ahead always.

4. Make it positive: Your goal statement should deal with what you want to do and not the things you do not want to do.

5. Frame action plan: Jot down all the steps and what you need to do in each step of the plan. Only by this you can realize if you are making progress.

6. Make it flexible: You should keep this in mind that setting goals is a way to achieve the target and not the target itself. As goals are always set over a time frame there should be enough flexibility to adapt to the changed situation but never losing the focus on achieving the target.

How to create SMART goals

- A Specific goal has maximum chances of achieving success. To frame this, you should take the help of the six Ws. You must question who is involved? What will be accomplished? Where it will be done? When it will be done? Which will be fulfilled? And why it should be done?

- The Measurable goals allow you to know your performance. For doing so you must ask questions like: How much?

How many? How to know if it is achieved?

- To make your goals Attainable you must chalk out various ways to make it happen including development in attitudes, skills, improved technologies and financial assistance.

- The goal set must be Relevant to your periphery of work. You can make it as high or as low you may wish for framing the long term and short-term objectives respectively.

- Nothing should be left for indefinite period as in such cases the goal set loses its importance and urgency. As such goals should always be Timed.

WORKING AGREEMENTS

Working agreements alleviate confusion and reduces risk

All of us shake our hands for so many reasons. But do you know how it started? Whether you believe it or not it started first to ensure one another that neither of them was carrying any weapon. And as the meaning of everything changes with time, handshaking is now evolved as a contractual symbol indicating complete agreement between the two persons.

It is now pertinent to ask if the handshake deals still carry some weight. Over the years I was also an ardent follower of handshaking principles. It never struck that it could be dishonored. But well, experience is the learning we all receive from our past mistakes and I am no exception too! Now whenever I do a job I put every detail in writing and get those signed by the concerned parties before starting the job. Now I have no fluctuation as the working agreements alleviate confusion.

The realm of promises

Promises are in fact contracts expressed by spoken communication and not written down. If there is an oral promise about doing something and finally not doing that, it is also a breach of contract with the only specialty that this is difficult to prove in the court of law. But when these are available in the written form it becomes easy to call for specific performance of the same.

The working agreements

The inherent advantage of this is that it not only states the promise made, but also serves as a token of proof. Being the promise and proof simultaneously working agreements are more ironclad than oral contracts as these are made by and between the parties. As these contain the signature of both the parties it ensures that both parties clearly understand what is stated and are committed to comply the stipulations.

The zone of trouble

When it comes to one person's spoken words against the others, it may be difficult to find the justice in case of any broken promises. Working agreements may also cause future problems because of poor drafting. But it is still better for minimizing the risks of violation.

Advantages of working agreement

Let me tell you some of the inherent advantages of working agreement in the following lines.

- Preventing amnesia: Jotting down the deals means you must keep nothing in mind and so there is no chance of a slip causing confusion and conflict.

- Easy reference: Working agreements help to provide handy reference for answering any queries about the details.

- Planning the work: Putting details in writing is a great way to have a well thought plan about the job and the responsibility of the parties.

- Encouraging consistency: Having everything on paper means providing uniform set of information to all concerned and thus increases consistency of performances.

- Promoting harmony: Working agreements prevent disputes. These also act as a guideline and play a very vital role in resolving potential disputes or confrontation.

- Easier enforcement: Working agreements are easier to enforce because of its absolute legality.

- Sealing the deal: Working agreements seal the deal in respect of time, cost, commitment, responsibility, compensation thus lead to smooth implementation.

WORK
BOOK

MARKETING ONE PAGE PLAN TEMPLATE DEFINITIONS

Target Market

Target market is basically the potential buyers to whom a business wants to sell its products or services, to which the business diverts all its marketing campaigns and those who are likely to buy products or services from the business. Marketing strategy of the business is based on this element and this can be separated by several factors like location, buying capacity and demographics.

A niche market is the subset of Target Market. There can hardly be any business that can cater to the needs of all people meeting all their requirements. As a matter of fact, narrow marketing has greater chances to grow. Target Niche may be defined as the part of the target market where the business concentrates to separate it from competitors. This is a subset of the Target market on which a specific product is focused. There is no existence of target niches in the market, but these are created by the business identifying the requirements. This makes the business cost effective and helps to operate more effectively.

Positioning Statement

Also referred to as brand positioning statement, it is a succinct expression of how a given product or service fulfills the needs of the consumers better than the competitor brands. There are four elements to this: Target customer, referential frame, Point of difference and convincing reasons. A good positioning statement helps to identify the appropriate niche and to get established in the market.

Offering to Customers

In marketing offering to customers means your ways to make them understand the sum total of benefits they receive for associated payment in using your product or services. It helps to enhance the customer's perception of your products or services affect their decision for purchasing from you.

Price Strategy

It refers to the method a business applies for pricing their products or services. This considers various segments like paying capacity, condition of the market, action taken by the competitors, costs and margins. There are many types of price strategy such as discount pricing, penetration pricing, price skimming, product life cycle pricing and competitive pricing.

Distribution

It is the process that a business employs for spreading the products or services throughout the market, for consumption, directly or through intermediate channels. This is critical for every business and the businesses moving faster and wider than the competitors make more impacts and enjoys greater margin.

Sales Strategy

A sales strategy focuses on the efforts of a business for improving sales focusing on the existing and potential target customers and communicates with the market in appropriate ways. It includes a plan that helps the product to gain advantage over the competitors. All successful sales strategies have a defined sales plan, sales activities, targets and timelines.

Service Strategy

It aims to optimize the after sales service that a business provides by coordinating components, service personnel and service cost. Such strategies help to gain customer loyalty through improved after sale service performance.

Promotion Strategy

It is the process of getting the brand public for attracting potential customers. It uses a blend of advertising, personal selling and public relation for promoting the products or services. The promotion strategies differ depending of the specific needs of the business, but all of them strive to enhance brand awareness and demand.

Market Research

It is the organized effort employed by a business for collecting information about the target markets and customers. It includes social and opinion research analyzing and interpreting the information gathered for effective decision making. It helps you reduce the risks and helps to focus on the resources where those will be most effective for producing desired results.

Other Component of your Marketing Plan

Any marketing plan has five 'P's: product, price, promotion, people and place and the other components of marketing plan include mission & vision statement, situational analysis, budget and action plan, metrics, monitoring of results.

YOUR COMPANY NAME HERE 2018

Category	"THEME" Strategy
Target Market	
Positioning Statement	
Offering to customers	
Price Strategy	
Distribution	
Sales Strategy	
Service Strategy	
Promotion Strategy	
Marketing Research	
Any other component of your marketing plan	

PAWS Doggie Day Care 2018

Marketing Theme: Fun without the Sun	
Category	**Strategy**
My reason for existence:	To provide pet owners within the city of Springfield a safe and fun place for their pets
What sets my business apart from the rest:	An indoor pet park and pay-land
My ideal customer is:	1. Springfield professionals working in the 10 mile radius 2. 3.
What's most important to my ideal customer when they are buying what I'm selling	1. That their pets are safe 2. Pets can have fun in any weather 3. Exercise
What I want to accomplish this year:	• Lease a building • Recruit customers •
The top 4 things that are going to get me there:	1. Direct mail in nearby developments 2. Drop-offs in office parks 3. Open house events 4. Social Media Marketing
How much will each program contribute to my revenue/profitability:	1. Mail - 30% 2. Drop offs - 15% 3. Open House - 25% 4. Social Media Marketing 30%
What will trigger my ideal customer to think of me:	• Being stuck at work and pet needs to be let out • •
Programs I am running to reach my goal	1. Online Advertising 2. 3.
How much money will I need to get it done?	1. $2,500 2.

BOOK DISCUSSION QUESTIONS

1. What would you say are the top three skills needed to be a successful entrepreneur?

2. Have you decided what business you would like to start?

3. Who is your Target Market?

4. Who is your Target Niche?

5. How did you come up with the idea for your business?

6. What make your business different from others?

7. What colors would you like for your Logo?

8. After reading Boss Up, what advice will you give to an Entrepreneur before starting their business?

9. What do you want your business to be known for?

10. What business or entertainer has a compelling brand?

ABOUT THE AUTHOR

Marilyn Bryant-Tucker, MBA, EGCBA is the owner of MBT Marketing Solutions, and can offer quite a wide range of high- quality marketing services such as event marketing, branding, communication and much more. She is a certified marketer whom has great zeal for helping micro and small business owners grow their business, with her wealth of knowledge and experience. Bryant-Tucker is committed to giving the best of marketing services with a focus on reasonably prices, top-quality marketing and publicity services. She is a native of Rocky Mount, North Carolina, but for the past 29 years of her life resided in Raleigh, North Carolina.

Marilyn holds an MBA in Marketing, Executive Graduate Certificate Business Administration and has pursued Doctoral Studies in Marketing. She earned her Master's Business Administration in Marketing from Strayer University in 2011 and an Executive Graduate Certificate.

Made in the USA
Las Vegas, NV
26 February 2022